ONE SUMMER IN YOUR SHOES

Laura Latimer

Copyright © 2025 Laura Latimer

Table of Contents

Chapter 1 - MISCHIEF 1

Chapter 2 - CHARLES' HOUSE 13

Chapter 3 - JOE'S HOUSE 18

Chapter 4 - CHARLES' HOUSE 24

Chapter 5 - JOE'S HOUSE 34

Chapter 6 - SWOPPING NOTES 50

Chapter 7 - POP THE QUESTION 59

Chapter 8 - SCOTLAND 65

Chapter 9 - I'M HOME 78

Chapter 1 - MISCHIEF

Minx was angry. When Minx was angry, anything could happen. Sudden gusts of wind blowing children off their bikes. Pine cones in their hundreds coming off a tree and hitting someone at full force, if they annoyed her, or even if they didn't. Objects disappearing, then reappearing. If Minx wasn't angry, the events were more mischievous than cruel. Cups sliding along a table, papers lifting then falling, books that opened themselves, cats or dogs that seemed to talk; that sort of thing. Minx always misbehaved; that was the nature of being a Goblin. What made her really angry were the 'Godlins'. There were six of them and they had changed their name from Goblins to 'Godlins', because they wanted to be nicer. In Minx's opinion, they thought too much of themselves. They wanted to become nice and do nice things for humans. They even changed their names, Mayhem to May, Chaos to Cha, Tricky to Ricky, Devious to Devi, Sneaky to Ky, and Whirlwind to Breezy. They wanted Minx to be the same, but she wasn't having any of it.

"I'm not going to become good. What's the point of being a Goblin, if you can't do bad things."

Now you may be thinking Goblins don't exist, because you can't see them. Well, that's because they don't want to be seen. What would be the point of doing mischief if you can be seen doing it. Goblins can disappear and reappear whenever they like. Another thing, they can become really, really angry, and when they do their powers increase. If they become really, really angry the trouble they can cause is immense. Even they don't know what they can be capable of. Whatever they are thinking of at the time can become a reality.

Minx was in that frame of mind, as the 'Godlin' Goblins had been giving her grief, threatening to lock her in the dungeon prison if she didn't change. The Godlins lived in the Keep. It was in ruins in real time, but Goblins live in what could be described as a parallel world. Their version of the Keep was not a ruin, but a solid building, with roof, windows, gatehouse and an underground dungeon. If humans visited it all they saw was a ruin, a pile of stones, nothing more. Minx was also hiding from them. It was easier to hide from them when they were being nice because they were not as powerful. She was hiding on a park, there were swings, climbing frames, and a large football pitch. It was empty, as all the kids were at school, or so she thought. Leading off from the park was a swathe of houses, built in the 1950's, all looking the same. Beyond that were three plain looking blocks of flats. The park was at the bottom of the hill, that lead down from them, with terrace houses closest to the park. On the other hill, going up, were the big houses, all different, with big drives, some with electric gates. On the driveways, you could have fitted one of the houses from the other side. Some even had swimming pools, which the wind filled with leaves carried by the violent winds that blew down the valley, blowing straight from the North Sea.

The town of Melby sprawled in both directions. Among it were a hospital, a supermarket, several warehouses or factories, and schools.

Now, Goblins live for many years, and Minx had seen the changes over those many years, including the schools. One was a large, sprawling modern building complex, that taught over 600 pupils. There was also an older Victorian building, where the rich people sent their children, from the age of three to eighteen. It was as if someone had drawn a line through the town.

This particular day, Minx was sitting under a tree by the football pitch, when a large group of lads, about 20, appeared with a football, and began to play a game. It was rough, and physical. Two lads, one called Smeggs, the other Joe, ordered everyone around. Of the two Joe seemed the more in charge. The game, which involved quite a lot of fouling and swearing, was still quite good natured, in a camaraderie sort of way. About twenty minutes in another group of lads appeared. About the same age, 12-13. There were about fifteen of them, but the swagger about them was different. They held their heads high, backs straight. Their hair was immaculate, their t-shirts, or shirts, clearly not from any old shop. At the front of them, was a lad with a blazer.

"What do we have here?" He called. "It's the council estate kids, trying to play football. I'm even amazed they know how to play, judging by the looks of them."

Smeggs and Joe, who were trying to get the ball off each other at the time, stopped and turned to face the interlopers. Ten minutes later the football match turned into a fight, kicking, hitting, punching, between the two sides.

Minx had actually done nothing to cause this. Invisibly she moved, the anger welling up even more inside her, as Joe was about to punch the lead boy of the other group. Minx thought, what if they swopped bodies, and lived each other's lives for thirty days. As Joe's punch neared the boy's face Minx shouted "NOW."

The world went into slow motion, then stopped, apart from the two boys.

Joe was aware of the swing of his punch. The next thing he knew was that he saw himself throwing a punch that hit him square across the jaw.

"What the _____," he said.

The two boys stopped and looked at each other. Everyone else was frozen in mid-fight.

Joe looked down at himself, then at what was really himself. His voice sounded different. What was Joe, looked at him, then pulled him away, through the frozen figures, to the side of the pitch. Then everyone unfroze and the fighting continued.

Minx appeared before them, clicked her fingers, and the three found themselves on the path that led away from the park, surrounded by trees. Nobody else could see them.

"What's going on?" the boy asked.

"You've swopped bodies." Minx answered.

"What! Why?" Joe said.

"Because I can do that, though actually I didn't know I could."

"You mean, I have to be him." The boy shouted.

"Yes, for thirty days."

"And I have to be him, that snobby, rich kid?"

"Yes."

Both boys reached to grab Minx, but she disappeared, then reappeared behind them.

"What the _____." Which was Joe's favourite phrase of the moment.

"You can't do this." Charles said, which was the other boy's name.

"You'll just have to live with it." Minx said.

"What are you? Who are you?" Joe shouted.

"Me. I'm a Goblin, a mischief maker. But it's not going to be forever." She said proudly. "Just enough to make your lives interesting."

"But I don't want to be him." Joe said.

"And I don't want to be him." Agreed Charles.

"Well, then you've agreed on something."

"So, how do you know when we will change back?" Joe asked an intelligent question.

"It will just happen, just like that." Minx then disappeared, then reappeared at Joe's side.

"One day, in thirty days, hey presto, you will be back as yourselves again."

Joe did a mental calculation. Today was the 28th of July, that would make it, possibly, the 26th of August. Charles, couldn't work it out in his brain, because, truth to tell, he wasn't good at mental arithmetic, for all his parents had spent on his education, he wasn't that bright.

"The 26th of August," Joe announced.

"Oh yes, you humans have calendars, and dates. Us Goblins just count the moon's and sun's appearance. Our idea of time is a bit different from yours."

"Are you going to take any responsibility?" Joe asked.

"What for?" Minx replied.

"Us, your experiment."

"Oh, this isn't an experiment. It's mischief, and mischief has no rules."

"But you just gave us a rule, that it is only for thirty days." Joe argued.

"My, you're a bright one." Minx replied.

"And you can't break that rule."

"No, you got me there."

"And I'm sure you'll be watching us."

"Well, yes, occasionally."

"Because you want to see how your mischief turns out."

"Well, yes."

"So, if we call for you, will you appear?"

"Do you want me to?"

"Yes, we do." Shouted Charles, having tried to follow the conversation.

"And do you have a name? Or do we make up a name for you…like Twinkletoes."

"Or Crabby." Charles said.

"Or Puffball."

"Macaroni."

"Curry."

The two boys bantered names, back and forth, until Minx got fed up.

"Minx," she said, eventually. "Okay. I'll appear if you call, but only within five miles of here."

"Why?"

"Because of the Goblin Kingdom. We each have our districts, and we can't go into another Goblin's territory, otherwise they might eat us."

"It seems," Joe observed, "that Goblins have more rules than you care to admit."

"I'm going." Minx said. "Don't call me that often, or I'll just ignore you."

With that she disappeared.

The two boys looked at each other.

Charles said "Your house or mine."

"Yours." Joe said.

And off they went.

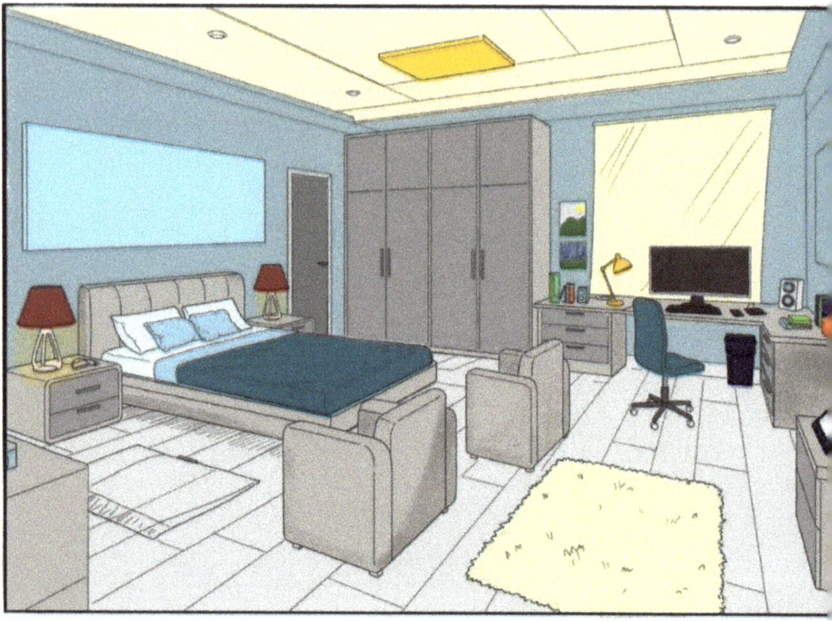

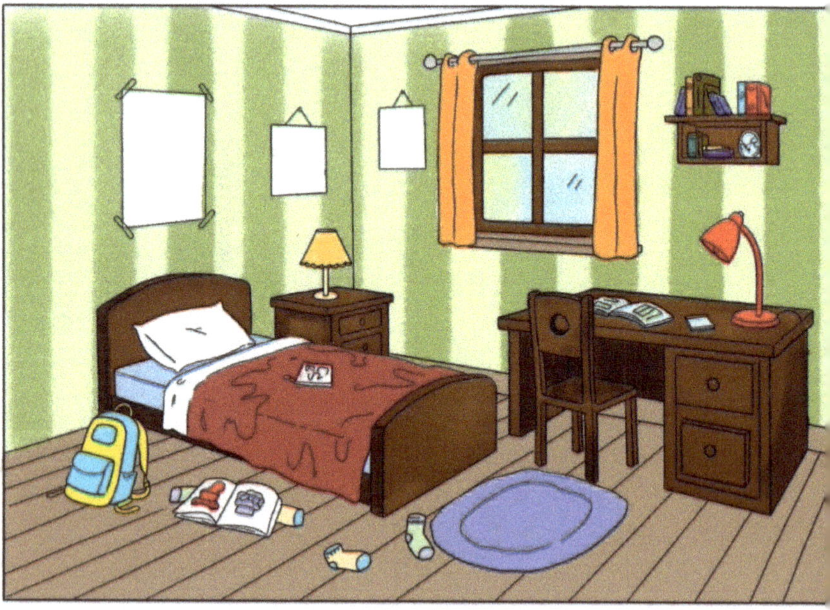

Chapter 2 - CHARLES' HOUSE

Charles' house was nearly at the top of the hill. It was a steep walk. Up the road, then they turned round a bend. Joe gasped. The house was huge, and there were big metal gates in front. Charles, who was now Joe, keyed in four numbers into a side gate, and opened it.

Can you remember 8421? The number is halved each time."

"Yes, I can," said Joe.

There was a paved area for cars, then a shrubbed area with flower beds leading up the path to the front door. The real Charles opened the door.

"You leave the door unlocked?"

"Well, yes, Edie, Mrs Johnson, the housekeeper is always here in the day. She leaves at 7 pm."

They walked into a large hallway, to the right was a staircase.

"Come on, let's go to my bedroom." Charles said.

There was a long corridor upstairs, with lots of pictures on the walls. Charles walked briskly, Joe trotting behind. Charles opened the last door at the end of the corridor, into his bedroom. His bedroom was so big. There was a bed on the left, two armchairs facing a wall, that had a large tv on it. To the right of the bed there was a desk with a laptop, a pile of Wii games, a box of cables and controls, next to it.

There was a small bookcase. With a small selection of books. Charles didn't seem much of a reader. One wall had fitted wardrobes, and a chest of drawers. In the corner of the room was another door. Charles opened the door. There was a small shower room, sink and toilet. In the other corner was a shelf unit with all sorts of electronic toys, cars, robots, a CD player and radio.

Charles opened up the chest of drawers and began packing a backpack with some underpants and socks.

"What you doing?" Joe asked.

"Well, I'll probably have to wear your clothes, but I'm not going to wear your socks or underpants."

He then went to a desk drawer and took out two notebooks and thrust one at Joe.

"What's that for?" asked Joe.

"We're going to write everything you do down, because when we swop bodies back, we're going to have to know everything we've done, so write everything down. Right, now follow me."

He then opened the bedroom door, down the stairs, Joe following, into the lounge.

But his mother saw a strange boy charging into the room, with her son following.

"Charles, who's this?"

Joe as Charles, pulled Joe forward.

"I'm Joe, I mean, this is Joe, my friend."

"How do you do Joe, I'm Charles' Mother. I've not met you before."

Joe said, "Oh, we met playing football."

He then said, "We've got to go back to my house. What time would you like Charles back home?"

"Supper is at 6 pm, so send him back then."

Joe beckoned to Charles to follow him, hoping he would not be so timid.

Then they exited through the front door. When they got outside the house, Joe, who was Charles, said "Get your act together."

"What?"

"Don't act like a dummy, you're me, take charge."

"But!"

"But nothing. Now let's go to yours."

Chapter 3 - JOE'S HOUSE

Joe and Charles walked down the hill, through the park where the fight happened. The fighting boys had long dispersed as both sets of boys knew when to run when they heard the police sirens. Some stayed to continue to play football, Joe found out later, just to give the impression that all was well. They had gone home now. The police had been satisfied that no crime had been committed, the disturbance over, and left shortly after. Life went back to normal, except for the two boys.

They then entered the sprawl of the housing estate, past Joe's school, to a block of flats. There was no security on the front door. Joe, climbed up two flights of smelly concrete stairs, with Charles, as Joe, following behind.

"Give me your key," Charles said.

Joe fished in his trouser pocket and drew out a Yale key.

"Open the door." Joe gave his namesake the key.

Charles did as he was told by the bossy Joe. They entered into a small entrance hall, with a place to hang coats, several cupboard doors. There was a kitchen to the right, a sitting room straight ahead, then several doors, one led to a bathroom, the other three must be bedrooms. The end one, Joe entered, was tiny. There was a bed, a bedside cabinet, bookshelves, a rail with clothes on it, and a small chest of drawers. A box on the floor had shoes in it.

"This is my room," Joe said to his replacement.

"It's tiny."

"Well, yours is so big, but this is how it is, your home for thirty days."

Joe sat on the bed, and Charles did the same. Joe then opened one of the drawers, took out some socks and pants, and thrust them into a backpack. He then added a book or two, then zipped it up.

Then a disembodied voice said, "Joe, is that you?"

Joe mouthed to Charles, "Say yes."

"Yes."

"Come out, it's time to make some tea."

"Who's that?" Charles asked.

"Maggie, my older sister. Come and meet her."

Both boys came out.

"Oh, you've got a friend over."

"This is Charles." Charles said.

It was weird to be introducing yourself, but he was getting more used to it, not being himself. If that was possible.

"Ooh, a posh name. Charles. Anyhow Mum left some stew in the fridge, to heat up, then there's some cakes in the tin. Just take your half. I'll eat mine a bit later."

Both boys looked at each other.

"In a bit." Joe said. "We've got some things to talk about."

He pulled the other Joe back into the bedroom. He then began to write furiously notes on a piece of paper, and thrust a bit of paper to Charles. On it was a list of family names. Joe wrote.

Mum Josie Acton, nurse.

Sister… Maggie, 16

Birthday 10.10.2010.

Then gave the piece of paper to Charles.

"Is that it? What about your dad?"

"I don't have one."

"Everyone has a dad."

"Well, I don't. I mean, I don't know who he is."

Joe, who was Charles, let out a loud "What!" He had never met anyone who didn't know who their dad was.

"That's the way it has always been."

"Now you write the same."

Charles wrote

Dad… James

Mum… Abigail

Sister…. Lucy, 8 years old.

Mrs Johnson, Edie, housekeeper

Our surname… Barclay

Code 8421

Birthday 6.2.2011.

Maggie then was heard to shout through the door.

"Joe, come on, it's Mum on the phone."

Charles asked. "Could she not have phoned you on your mobile?"

Joe laughed.

"I don't have a mobile… yet. Go and speak to my Mum."

They went out of the room, and Charles took the phone nervously.

"Darling, could you go and buy some milk and bread. I won't be home until late, so make sure you eat your supper."

Both boys went to the corner shop, Joe, money in hand, then they parted ways, both going to their new existence, both scared.

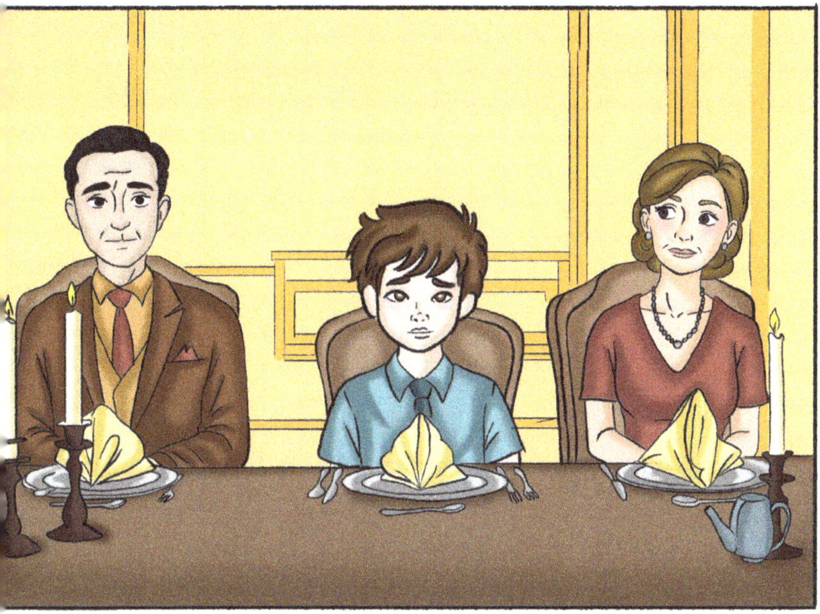

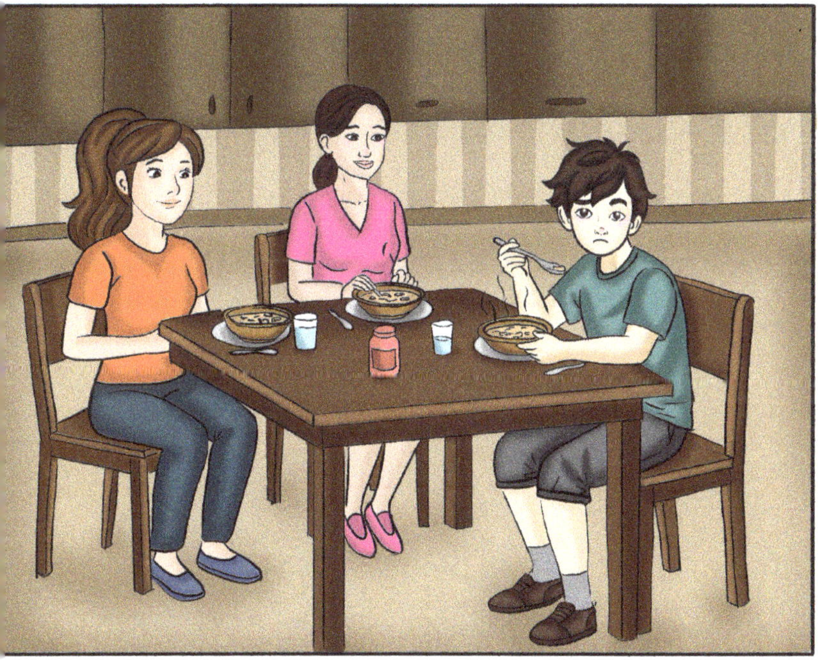

Chapter 4 - CHARLES' HOUSE

Joe kept muttering to himself all the way up the hill, "Remember I am Charles."

He actually knew nothing about Charles, or not much, except that he was rich. Joe's demeanour changed at that thought. In Charles' bedroom, there was a Wii and a television. There was always a good cooked meal. Not having to worry whether it was beans or beans on toast for supper. He also had Charles' mobile phone. Joe was the only one of his social group of friends that didn't have a mobile phone. Also, the only one not to have a dad. Even Carl had a divorced dad, who had them at weekends. Oh, and Sam, whose dad was often away as he was a long-haul truck driver, but he did see him sometimes.

Using the codes Charles gave him, Joe entered his new home. As he entered, he saw Mrs Johnson. She was Carl's grandmother. 'What's she doing here?' He thought, then he remembered Charles saying something about a housekeeper.

"Hello Mrs Johnson," he said.

"What happened to Edie?"

"Edie?"

"Yes, you and Lucy always call me Edie, so what's with this Mrs Johnson lark?"

"Sorry, Edie."

"Anyway, go and wash your hands and come down for supper. It will be served at 6 on the dot."

Joe ran upstairs to the bedroom, threw down his bag, and then went looking for where the meal was to be had.

Charles' mum and dad were seated on one side of the table, Lucy, his sister, on the other side. Joe sat down on the vacant chair.

Mrs Johnson placed a large glass dish with a shepherd's pie on the table, plus two serving dishes, one with carrots and one with peas and beans. Charles' dad served the food. Mrs Johnson had made such a large amount of food they couldn't eat it all. Joe also ate a good helping of everything.

"My goodness," Charles' mum said, "You've eaten more vegetables than you usually do."

"Well, it's all so good."

Mrs Johnson took the dishes away, then brought out an apple pie and custard. Joe helped himself to another glass of water. All the tumblers on the table were matching, all the food served on white plates with matching bowls. The cutlery was all the same, unlike at Joe's house, where nothing matched. The glasses were ones they had picked up from the street, that people had left on walls, or in corners. They cleaned them thoroughly and used them every day. Joe couldn't see Charles' parents doing such a thing.

After they ate dinner, Mrs Johnson cleaned away everything. Joe hadn't got used to the fact that he could call Carl's grandma Edie. Charles' mum, dad, and Lucy went into the sitting room. Joe followed Edie into the kitchen, where he saw her put the leftover food into the fridge.

"There's quite a lot of food left over," he said.

"Oh, I expect I will have to throw it away tomorrow," Edie replied. "It's such a waste."

"Why don't you take it home?" he asked.

"I'm not allowed too," Edie answered. "Only on rare occasions."

Edie loaded the dishwasher and made sure the kitchen was immaculate.

"Time to go now. I'll see you at breakfast."

Edie left through the back door.

Joe looked around the kitchen, looking in the drawers. He then found a drawer with plastic boxes in. 'I can put the leftover food in here and take it to my house tomorrow. Mum would just love some of this,' he thought, and Maggie. He wondered how Charles was coping.

He then went to the sitting room. Charles' dad was watching a serious documentary.

"Lucy," Joe said, "do you want to play some games on the Wii?"

"But you don't usually like me playing with you. You get annoyed with me."

"Well, not today. Come on, let's go up to my room. I don't want to play on my own."

Joe loaded Wii Sports onto the screen and played different games with Lucy, sometimes allowing her to win.

Charles' mum then came up to the room at about 8.30. "Time for you to have a bath Lucy, and get ready for bed."

Lucy disappeared to her own room.

"Do you want to play, Mum?"

"You'll have to show me what to do, I can't quite remember."

Joe went through the instructions, and they played a few games of tennis.

"That was fun. We must do this more often. Now, what are you going to do tomorrow, in the school holidays?"

"I've got a friend I'm going to see, and spend the day with him."

"Well, just let Edie know. Your dad and I both have work. You must also work on your maths. Your results from school were not good at all. Use the books we bought for you."

"Yes mum."

Joe laughed to himself. So, Charles was really bad at maths. Maths was one of the subjects at school that he was good at. He'd show Charles a thing or two.

"Oh, and here's your pocket money for the week."

Charles' mum gave him £25. Joe was amazed. £25 a week. He was lucky to get £5 a month.

Joe shut down the Wii, then went downstairs.

"Don't forget we're going to Scotland. In two weeks time." Dad said to Charles.

"Scotland?" Joe queried.

"Yes, did you not remember?"

"It slipped my mind."

"It will be so good to have a holiday. Work has been so hard. I really need a break."

"Can I bring a friend?"

"A friend. Which one?"

"He's called Joe."

Joe thought it wasn't really fair to have the holiday, when it was Charles holiday, not his. He had never really ever been away. Sometimes he went to his grandparents near Skegness with Maggie.

"I've not heard you mention Joe before?"

"Oh, he's a new friend."

"Talk to your mother. If it's okay with her, then it's fine with me."

Joe thought he'd wait until he spoke to Charles tomorrow. They had agreed to meet up at the park. Joe sat near Charles' dad, who seemed to be a quiet, reserved man. He looked like Charles, or rather, Charles looked like him.

His dad then said to him. "I think we need to get you a maths tutor. You can't get through life without getting a good result in maths. Maybe an English tutor to, though those results weren't as bad."

Joe didn't know what to say. In reality, Joe was good at both subjects. Maybe being at a local comprehensive school wasn't bad, he thought. If I had a chance to be at a fee-paying school, would I academically be any better? His teachers always thought he was bright. Maggie also did well at school. He wished his mum could afford something like that.

"That sounds like a good idea," Joe replied.

"You didn't say that last time, in fact, you said nothing at all, just stormed off to your bedroom."

"Oh. I mean, sorry."

Charles' mum came downstairs.

"It's getting late Charles, time for bed."

"Dad says to ask you if I can bring a friend to Scotland. I want to bring that boy Joe, who you saw earlier today."

"Well, if his parents agree. What do they do?"

"It's only his mum. She's a single parent. She works as a nurse at the local hospital."

"Should I phone her and ask?"

"Well, I could give her your number, but can I ask him first?"

"Okay, but ask soon."

"I'll do it tomorrow, but I'm sure he'll say yes, and I'm sure his mum will say yes as well."

Joe then went upstairs after saying goodnight. Before he went to bed, he wrote lots in his notebook, all under different headings, with bullet points. It certainly had been an eventful day. He then drew a cartoon of Minx, and an arrow through Minx's heart, with blood spurting out. Then he went to sleep.

Chapter 5 - JOE'S HOUSE

Charles said goodbye to Joe at the shop after having bought milk and bread, then he went back to Joe's house. The house was empty when he got back. Maggie had gone out to see her boyfriend. Charles took the stew out of the fridge, put half in a bowl, and microwaved it for two minutes, then sat at the kitchen table and ate it. He wished he were at home. Then he went looking for cakes, opening various tins. He eventually found them and ate two of the better-looking ones. He thought the stew was nice, but he felt lonely. He switched on the telly and watched 'The One Show.' Maggie returned, ate her stew, then washed up. Charles couldn't ask her, 'What does Joe do in the evening?' Maggie then got some DVDs out and they watched a thriller with Morgan Freeman. Joe's mum arrived back just before 10 pm, with some doughnuts and a bottle of lemonade. Totally bad for you, but so good, Charles thought.

He went to bed after writing up a few scrawled sentences in the notebook, with the date.

The next morning, Joe's mum knocked on the door to get him up.

"Bathroom's free," she called. Charles ran into the bathroom and made sure he locked the door. There were three towels on the towel rail, one pink with green flowers, one cream with embroidered flowers, and a plain blue one. Charles assumed that the blue one was the towel he had to use. He had a quick shower, then dashed back to Joe's room, chose some clothes from the limited selection, put his old clothes in the laundry basket and came out. On the table in the kitchen were three different boxes of cereal, a bottle of milk and a sugar bowl. Three bowls and plates were in the centre of the table, with some cutlery, a tub of butter and a jar of marmalade.

Charles poured out some cornflakes, added milk and sugar. Joe's mum put a cup of tea down on the table and Charles started to drink it.

"You haven't put sugar in," she said.

How was I supposed to know? He thought.

"I'm trying to give up sugar," Charles replied.

"Good luck with that, I hope you can."

Maggie came to the table, and Joe's mum sat down, after bringing six pieces of toast.

Charles took two and added butter and marmalade.

"Chores day today." Joe's mum announced.

"Joe, if you can do all the rubbish bins, it's a general rubbish collection this week, then hoover all the rooms. Maggie, can you dust, then clean the bathroom. Also, bring your laundry baskets into the kitchen, and I'll do the clothes wash.

Chores, thought Charles. 'I don't do chores.' This was turning into his worst nightmare. After breakfast Joe's mum gave Charles a binbag and he went round all the rooms emptying the rubbish into the bag. Then came into the kitchen and put it on the floor.

"Take it out to the chute, there's a love," she said.

The chute, where was that? Charles went out the front door, following Joe's mum's arm. Fortunately, he spotted some other people in the corridor pulling open a chute, and pushing several bin bags in. Charles did the same. When he returned Joe's mum said, "I've put Henry in the lounge." Henry? Was Henry a dog? He went into the lounge. Oh, Henry was a big, fat, round red vacuum cleaner.

"This is a first" he said aloud. He found the plug socket, switched on the green switch and began hoovering.

"Don't forget under the sofa and chairs," Joe's mum called out.

Fortunately, it wasn't a difficult job, and he moved onto the other rooms. Joe's mum's room was really tidy. Maggie's room was a different matter. He picked up crisp packets off the floor, but clothes were lying all over the floor as well. He threw them onto the bed, as well as bags, books, and some other things, when a pack of cigarettes fell out from one of the bags. He shoved them back in one of the bags. It was none of his business.

Maggie came in then, to collect her laundry. She saw the pack of cigarettes in the top of one of her bags.

"They're not mine, "she said. "They're Aidan's."

"Aidan?"

"Yes, his mum has taken to searching his bag to see if he's got any fags, so I'm looking after them."

"Oh yes, I really believe that."

Maggie whacked him round the head. "Shut it, or I'll really beat you up."

So, this was what having an older sister was like. Nothing like his sweet sister Lucy.

"You wouldn't dare. I'll tell mum."

"Since when did you turn into a snitch? Be quiet or I'll tell mum what you did with her favourite cushion, when you were sick all over it."

"Ugh."

"Washing it, by flushing it with toilet water to get the sick off. I saw you."

Charles didn't know what to say, so he said nothing.

"Good," Maggie said. "Just keep quiet, and we'll both be better off."

She then took the laundry basket to the kitchen. Charles finished hoovering her room, the corridor and then took Henry into the kitchen.

Maggie called through to Charles.

"Smeggs is at the door."

Who on earth was Smeggs? Charles thought to himself, as he went to the door.

A boy his age was standing at the door, football held in the crook of his arm.

"I'm bored" said Smeggs, "do you want to come and shoot goals?"

Maggie was standing behind Charles.

"Go," she said, "You've done the jobs for today. Hi Smeggs."

"Hi Maggie, how're things with Aidan?"

What's this with the Aidan thing, Charles thought? Why is Smeggs asking?

"Tell my cousin to be good, and not to rifle through my football cards, looking for ones to pinch. I'll kill him if he does."

"Tell him yourself."

"He'll beat me up, like he always does."

Charles looked at Smeggs. He wasn't exactly tiny, or weak, and definitely looked mean. Maybe that was because of his short-cropped hair, thin eyes, on a round face.

Smeggs and Charles walked down to the park. A few parents were playing with their young children on the equipment. There was one dog walker.

The boys went to the goal posts at the far end of the park. Smeggs gestured Joe to go into goal. What Smeggs didn't realise was that Charles was actually really good at football. He didn't know what Joe was like, but there were two things Charles was good at, scoring goals and saving goals. So much so that he played for the school team. He was determined not to let Smeggs win anything. In his determination to win, he didn't spot Minx at first, who was sitting on a branch of a tree, to the right of the goal. Minx waved at him. Out of the corner of his eye he saw that Minx was going to perform a magic spell on Smeggs. Charles turned to face her.

"Don't you dare", he mouthed.

Minx laughed, but then put her hand down, as if to say 'Okay, you win.'

Smeggs dribbled the ball a bit, then placed the ball about six yards from the goal and shot. Charles caught the ball. Smeggs then shouted "Best of five."

Charles deflected the second. Smeggs wondered what was going on. Joe was usually easy to beat. The third shot went in the corner of the net, the fourth hit the left-hand post. The fifth soared, then froze in mid-air. Smeggs was also frozen, one foot off the ground. Everyone in the park was frozen too, except Charles.

"What are you doing?" Charles shouted.

"It looks like you don't need my help. I wanted to help. Now I'm miffed." Minx jumped down from her perch.

"I can take care of myself."

"Humph. This boy is not a nice boy. I see him all the time bullying other boys."

"That's why I'm going to show him."

"Well then, I won't help you."

"Help me, how?"

"By making him lose."

"He's probably going to lose anyway, against me."

"You're very sure of yourself."

"At this, yes."

"And what about Joe?"

"What about him?"

"This boy could give him a hard time, if you win."

"He needs to be shown, that I, as Joe, am not a pushover."

"I could make him fall, with a bump."

"Can you rewind?"

"I can."

"Then rewind to where he's standing up, about to shoot."

Charles watched as Smeggs moved backwards in time, back to his starting position. When he came to, Smeggs was confused, he was sure he had already kicked the ball. A dog barked in the distance, the sound of an ambulance siren could be heard, the world was unfrozen.

Smeggs kicked the ball. Charles made a small effort to save it, but it went in. Then they swopped positions.

Charles hit four perfect balls, one hard in the centre, one just below the top bar, and one in each corner. He was about to shoot the fifth, to a disgruntled Smeggs, when a figure appeared behind Charles.

"What's that posh kid doing here?" Smeggs said.

Charles turned. It was Joe, as Charles, of course. Joe pulled Charles away.

"What are you doing?"

"Beating him at his own game."

"Why are you friends with him?" Smeggs shouted.

"How did you know I was here?"

Joe pointed at Minx.

"She told me."

Charles scowled. "Interfering…."

"Don't make Minx angry. You don't know what will happen."

"Get on with it." Smeggs shouted.

Charles turned round, placed the ball and kicked. Smeggs stopped it, but it hit him right in his belly. Smeggs doubled up on the ground.

Joe ran over to his friend.

"Smeggs, are you okay?"

"Get off me, posh kid."

Charles came over. Smeggs, still winded, got up shakily.

"When did you get so good at this?"

The three boys stared at each other.

"Let's go and get an ice cream". Joe said, in an attempt to defuse all the pent-up anger.

"Is the rich kid paying?" Smeggs asked.

"Yes," said Charles. "He's paying."

Minx floated down from her perch and watched the three boys disappear round the corner. Suddenly she heard a voice behind her.

"I can see you're breaking the goblin rules, left, right, up, down and centre."

It was Sneaky, or Ky. Even though Ky had given up on being totally bad Ky still managed to be sneaky, creeping around in black, hiding, listening in, not to be trusted.

"And you never break the rules." Minx snapped back.

"Maybe, but not the ones that say don't let humans see you, rule number four, and rule number five, don't make friendships with humans. And not forgetting rule number one, always be mean when you create mischief."

"That's rule number two, not one. At least I still act like a proper Goblin. I still have all my powers."

"Yes, but if the Goblin Lords heard about what I've just seen and heard, they would banish you to some remote place."

"You'd report me, would you?"

"That's my nature."

"Then I'd report you back. When did you last use your Goblin powers to create mischief?"

"But I could lie, that's what I always do."

"Then I'd stage a contest, a trial, where you'd have to prove your powers."

"I would then fake it. I can still scare people."

Minx raised her fist, as if to punch Sneaky, who dodged.

"I've not reported you, or any of the Godlins, up to now. Rule number one of the Goblin code. Goblin kingdom first. Uphold your fellow Goblins." Minx said.

"I do that, just not you. You moved out from the Keep, to build your own little living space, that tree house. You've abandoned us."

"But you all abandoned Goblin ways, by wanting to become nice."

"It isn't like that."

"What is it like then?"

"This modern world. Humans stay at home more, on those things called 'computers', or they walk along the streets, with things in their ears. If you try and scare them, they can't hear you. Or they're on that communicator thing, talking loudly, but no other human nearby. They just don't act scared anymore. We've run out of ideas, after hundreds of years."

"What about the 'Manual of Mischievous Deeds'? Are there no good prompts?"

"We're tired. Bored, and don't see the point anymore."

"And being good is the way forward!"

"There's no challenge left. Less fun. And we're just stuck here, in Melby."

"Well, I know that, but I still find mischief to do."

"Aren't you the lucky one!"

"Don't report me. It will make things worse for all us Goblins, having interference from outside."

"Then I'll tell the others, Minx is friends with humans, and lets them see her."

"So, I can do mischief and spells on them. That's why."

"Move back into the Keep, and I won't tell."

"No. I like my tree house."

"Your room is still there."

"I don't want to."

"Then just wait and see, what I'll do to you."

"Do you see my fist? I'll create a punching spell, that will leave you as dark as your clothes."

Both Minx and Sneaky glared at each other, then Minx flicked her fingers and vanished. Sneaky gave a 'humph' then walked off, back to the Keep, before he too vanished. It was true that Minx had stronger powers.

Chapter 6 - SWOPPING NOTES

Charles spent the next morning doing chores. This time loading the washing machine, and washing up. He realised how much he took things for granted. His clothes always got clean, ironed, folded, and put in his drawers, by Edie. Cleaning the house, the same. Not having his computer was hard, not being able to play games. Instead, he enjoyed being with Maggie, and Joe's Mum, not spending the time alone. They were nice people, even though Maggie was rough with him, he liked the banter. Sitting on the sofa, watching movies, eating on your lap, and chilling. They didn't have much, but managed to have fun. There was a closeness that he didn't have at home. He thought about Lucy, how they lived, and how he could be more friendly with her. Not treating her just as an annoying little sister.

He looked at the clock. It was time nearly to meet Joe at the park.

"Can I go to meet a friend now?"

"Yes, job finished. I'm off work today, but doing the night shift. How about we get a McDonalds for lunch?"

Charles had never had a McDonalds.

"That would be good."

"Come home for twelve, and we'll all walk down."

"Can I bring a friend?"

"If you want to, but I don't know if I can stretch the money that far, but it might be possible."

"Oh, I think he's got money. Don't worry."

"That's good."

Charles made sure he'd got the house key, and took his wallet out of the bag. In it he had £50 and his bank card. The bank account had been opened when he was ten. He'd saved a bit each month so he could buy the latest Nintendo games when they came out.

With that, he left the house to wait for Joe at the park, also carrying the notebook, and his bag.

Joe was sitting on a swing, back and forth went his legs as he got higher in the air. There were a few dog walkers that occasionally walked past, the dogs barking at what was invisible air, maybe it was Minx? Otherwise, the park was deserted. The morning sunlight filtered through the poplar trees. The wet dew almost dissipated. He saw himself, the inhabited Joe, with the spirit of Charles, walking into the park. He wondered which bit of him really existed in the other body. Was it the mind, the soul, the personality? He had never really thought deep thoughts before. Maths was the influence, the rule, in how his brain worked, with formulas, rules, and only one answer. Now he supposed it was where the plus, minus, multiplication, division symbols fell, that determined the outcome of a sum. Actually, this was bigger than that. The fact that Goblins existed had just been something he read in fairy stories, not part of the real world. All these presuppositions, that this world was the only one, had crashed. There may even be life on other planets!

Charles didn't think like that. He saw it like a fantasy game. He wasn't even sure if he wasn't living in one of those games. That he'd been swallowed up by his computer. He saw himself on the swing, his body, and shouted out "Joe." Joe slowed down his swinging, put his feet on the ground and came to a halt. Charles sat down on the swing next to him.

They swopped notebooks. Charles read Joe's detailed notes. Joe read Charles' scrawled sentences.

Charles then laughed at the cartoon picture of Minx.

"By the way, your mum is going to take your sister and me to McDonalds. I said I was going to bring a friend, that's you."

"And your mum and dad are going to Scotland. I asked if I could bring a friend, that's you." He said, echoing Charles' words. "It didn't seem right to not let you come, as I'm the interloper."

"Will your mum let me, I mean, you go?"

"I should think so. We have to go and talk it over, with her?"

"How is it going, at my house?"

"Strange, but I like playing the Wii with your sister, and the food is really good."

"I felt a bit lonely. I was on my own for a few hours, then I had to do the chores this morning. I've never done that before. Edie usually does everything."

"Oh, yes, Saturday morning chores. I didn't warn you about them."

"Should we call Minx?"

"Why?"

"Why not?"

"Okay. Let's see is she'll come, like she said."

Joe called out first, then Charles.

"Minx."

"Minx."

Nothing happened.

"Oh well, that was for nothing." Then he tried to bark.

Minx suddenly appeared on the bench behind them.

"I'm here."

"We called you about five minutes ago."

"Well, I'm a tease. Why should I come straight away?"

"That's not fair." Joe said.

"Well, it's not about being fair, otherwise I'd be a Godlin."

"How do you explain what happened to us?" Joe asked. "Is it my soul that lives in him, my mind, my personality? What?"

"My, aren't we just trying to be too clever. Let's just say it's complicated and leave it at that."

"I'm not stupid."

"I'm not saying you are, but some things are beyond human explanation."

"You're toying with us." Joe shouted.

"I like toying with people. I've even been toying with your mum."

"My mum, why?"

"Cos, I like your mum, having seen her up close. And I'm not the only one."

"What do you mean?"

"Well, there's a guy at the hospital. I think he's a doctor, and he really likes your mum."

"Now you're messing with me again."

"Of course, and them! I thought I'd give her a helping hand."

"What?"

"I made her tip a patients wee all over his nice white coat, just by pushing her a little. It was fun. She then had to apologise so much to him, that she agreed to take her lunch break with him."

"So?"

"Then he wanted to see her again."

Joe didn't know what to say.

"I can read your mind, you know." Minx said. "You want a dad, so I thought I'd see what I could do about it."

"You're a meddling good for nothing, interfering pain in the butt." Joe yelled.

"I know. Isn't it wonderful?"

"I hate you."

"Even better."

Joe swung round to hit Minx, who disappeared, then reappeared the other side of Charles.

"Well, how's it going? It's been fun watching you."

"Watching us!" Charles exclaimed.

"Yes, popping in and out. Invisibly of course."

Minx did a little dance.

"Well, have you got anything to say to me? Otherwise, I'm disappearing."

Both boys said nothing.

"Oh well, I'm off then. Just call if you need me, and I may or may not come." With that Minx disappeared.

"I think we need to go back to yours." Charles said. "And talk to your mum."

Chapter 7 - POP THE QUESTION

"Mum, this is my friend Charles."

It was getting easier for them to introduce each other as the other person Joe realised. He also realised just how much he missed his mum. Today, out of her nurses uniform she wore jeans and a turquoise shirt. She tied back her long black hair into a loose ponytail. Joe had always thought his mum was pretty, better than some of the other mums.

"He lives up the hill, on the other side of town." Charles said.

"Nice to meet you." Joe said, pretending that this was the first time he had ever met her. It was odd, acting like this. He had to stop himself from bursting out giggling.

"Would you like some lemonade? I think we've got a bottle somewhere."

"Yes, that would be nice."

He followed his mum into the kitchen, and was about to open the kitchen cupboard where the motley collection of glasses were kept.

"You must be intuitive. How did you know I keep the glasses in there?"

'I must be more careful,' Joe thought. This is so hard. Charles entered the kitchen as well. Joe put out the glasses, and Josie, Joe's mum poured out the lemonade, then returned the bottle to one of the cupboards.

Joe waited for his mum to leave the kitchen, and took out the three plastic boxes of food, the leftover shepherd's pie, vegetables and apple pie from the night before. He showed Charles what he had done.

"What are you doing that for?" Charles, who was Joe, said.

"Not wasting food. Eat it for your supper tonight, and tell mum and Maggie it's there."

"Edie will go mad."

"Let me deal with that. I'll say I ate it all, or something like that."

Charles was amazed. How could this boy, Joe, be so cheeky? He wondered what else he was doing, at his home. Stealing food from the fridge and bringing it here. Did he think he was like Robin Hood, taking from the rich to give to the poor? He scowled at Joe, who didn't seem to notice.

They then went into the lounge. Charles spoke first.

"Charles' parent's have invited me to go to Scotland, on holiday with him. Can I go?" If he kept Joe in his sights as much as possible, less damage would be done.

Josie thought for a moment.

"I don't see why not. Have you got the dates?"

"The 10th of August to the 24th." Charles replied.

Josie looked in her diary, wrote the dates down.

"I shall need your parent's phone number, so I can call them to confirm all this."

Joe looked anxiously at Charles, then thought on his feet, because he knew he didn't know the number.

"I'll just go and get it," Charles dashed off to Joe's bedroom, found a piece of paper, opened Charles' phone, or his phone as it was, and scrawled down the number. He couldn't remember it himself either, but never thought it was his lack of skill in remembering numbers was a problem, because they were all stored on his phone. He then returned to the lounge and handed the paper over to Joe's mum.

"Maybe you can write down his parent's names on it for me."

Charles, scribbled down James and Abigail Barclay.

"What happened to you nice, neat, handwriting? I can only just about read it."

"Sorry Mum," Charles, said. "I was just writing it in a hurry."

Josie tucked the piece of paper into her wallet.

"Come on, let's go to McDonalds."

"Maggie," she called. "We're going."

Maggie appeared out of her bedroom, wearing a t-shirt and shorts, with pretty sandals. Charles, looked at her. Her long, dark hair flowed over her shoulders.

"I'm in love," he thought.

They walked out of the door, down the lift and into the blazing sunshine.

"One day I'm going to marry your sister."

Joe, hit him hard, across his back.

"Don't be stupid." Joe, said. "Get your act together."

They walked a mile to McDonalds, and Josie grabbed a table. She handed her purse to Charles, to pay for the food.

"I'll have a double cheeseburger, fries, and a coffee." Maggie ordered the same, but with a coke.

At the counter the boys placed their order, Charles said "I'll pay for this, keep your mum's money." He swiped his card on the machine, keyed in the pin, waited for the order, then returned to the table.

"By the way," Josie said, "I'm going out tonight for supper, with a friend, so I won't be home."

"A friend?" Maggie enquired.

"Yes, you lot can forage in the cupboard, can't you? "There's cans in the top one."

Joe and Charles looked at each other. Was she going on a date?

"It's a friend from work." Josie said.

The boys looked at each other. Yes, it was a date, their eyes spoke to each other, across the table.

Chapter 8 - SCOTLAND

In the intervening two weeks before the trip to Scotland Joe and Charles spent almost every day with each other, though there was the day Joe had to go to the dentist, and have some braces fitted, which Charles did not enjoy.

"Torture," was how Charles described it to Joe.

"What I did on your behalf. I deserve a medal. But then, I'm in love with your sister. She's so cool."

"Maggie, that's gross."

"She just thinks of me as her little brother, at the moment, but you never know."

Joe whacked him round the head with a maths book.

"Now, let's get on and help you with some maths."

Joe opened the book at division, which Charles struggled with. Actually, he struggled with everything in maths. Joe was about to discover something important about why Charles found maths so hard.

After trying to get Charles to do various sums he realised that Charles was confusing the number 5, with the number 2, the number 1 with the number 7, and the numbers 6 and 9.

"You know," he said, "I think you've got number blindness."

"What's that?" "I think it's called dys, dys, scal, calculia, or something like that. Your brain mixes up what you see. It's no wonder you find maths hard. There's a boy in my class just like it, and he gets extra help in maths, from Mrs Betts, who comes into class to help him. Don't you have anything like that, at your school?"

"No, they just dismissed me as being bad at maths."

"Well, I think you should ask your parents to pay for a proper assessment, when we get back to normal. You aren't stupid, you just can't help it."

"Maybe, I never realised that."

"I can help you a little, if I write the numbers in different colours, so 1 is green, 2 is orange, 5 is pink, 7 is blue, 6 is yellow, 9 is purple, and all the rest are in black or blue biro, that might help."

Joe wrote some sums for Charles and soon he began to get the answers right.

"I'll help explain it to your parents, when we get back to normal."

"Thanks Joe, I'm really grateful."

The following day Joe, with Lucy, and Charles' parents picked up Joe, who was Charles, from outside his block of flats. Maggie and Josie waved goodbye, watching as the people carrier disappeared out of sight.

Joe had never really left his home county before as they drove up the M1, M11, A1. It was all new to him. They stopped off the motorway for services, then crossed over to the west of the country, where his parents swopped drivers. Charles' mum was the better driving.

As the afternoon wore on, the miles passed among the beautiful scenery, they arrived at their destination. The cottage was in a remote place, on a flat piece of land, but surrounded by beautiful hills. The cottage had three bedrooms, a kitchen, large sitting room, ensuite shower rooms, plus an extra bathroom with a bath. There were large picture windows that overlooked the hills, fields of sheep, some highland cattle. To Joe it seemed that they were alone in this place, as he couldn't see any other houses.

Charles' mum and dad got everyone to unload the people carrier and bring everything into the cottage. Joe and Charles looked at their twin-bedded room and chose the bed they wanted. Then Lucy, Charles and Joe went exploring down the lane, specifically to look at the highland cattle. Lucy gave them names.

Charles' parents were really tired from the journey, with all the driving. Fortunately, supper that night was a meal that Mrs Johnson had prepared in advance, so it just needed heating up.

The following night Lucy, Charles and Joe explored the lane again, while Charles' parents prepared a meal. Lucy, after ten minutes, needed to run back to go to the toilet, not wanting to go behind a bush. Joe and Charles were left on their own. Joe ran across an open piece of ground, glad to be in such a wild place, Charles following close behind.

Joe, as he ran, ignored the fact that the ground under his feet was getting wetter, and wetter. He then got stuck, up to his knees in a bog.

Bog, in this case, was not where Lucy was headed, but an area of mud, very wet, which because of its softness cannot support the weight of whoever stands on it and they begin to sink into the ground so much that it is impossible to pull oneself out of it. Many hikers walking boots have disappeared in these bogs, if not whole children, leading people to speculate that a mythical creature swallowed them whole.

What Joe and Charles were to realise, as the sky became darker, and the sun began to set, was that such creatures were real. They had discovered that Goblins

existed, but what they were about to just encounter was much more scary.

Charles, who ran to try and help Joe suddenly stopped running, not because the ground was boggy. He had been jumping on clumps of grass. He stopped because a grey, mist-like creature rose up from behind Joe, and was pushing Joe further into the bog. Joe was screaming, Charles was yelling. Both boys were scared. Joe thought, as Charles, this was the end of his short life and how would he explain it to Charles' parents. Charles, as he watched himself being sucked into the bog, and not being able to do anything about it. How would he tell his parents that he, Charles, was gone, and that he would have to live as Joe for the rest of his life. Also, who was this grey creature?

At that moment, there was a large flash of light and Joe shot out of the ground, like a rocket, ten feet into the air, then slowed, came to a halt, then like a corkscrew, swizzled, twizzled, down to the ground, landing three feet from where he had been, landing on a safe piece of ground.

The grey creature melted away into the night air. Charles ran over to Joe.

"What was that?" he called out.

"It's a Boggart," another voice called out.

Joe and Charles turned round to see a figure, dressed in muddy green, trailing, raggedy clothes, with a pointy hat.

"Who are you?" Joe asked.

"Me, I'm a Boglin."

"And what's a Boglin?"

"Well, dumbie, it's a Goblin who lives in a bog, hence Boglin."

Joe had not yet recovered from his scary experience and was still shaking from fear, as well as the cold bog water. Charles was shaking because he was just scared.

"You're shaking, well you have just met a Boggart, and survived. A Boggart is a nasty creature. You don't want to meet one, though you did. They make children, like yourselves disappear in the bog, never to be seen again. But you two are different, you have a spell on you. I could sense it on the wind. You have a Goblin magic colour, and a sound, that you cannot see or hear, but we can. With a Goblin's promise, to make all things right again. That is how I could save you."

"You mean, if we didn't have the spell we wouldn't have been saved?" Joe asked.

"I would have saved any child if I could. I create mischief not harm. That is why I'm here."

"I've never shot up in the air like that before," Joe said. "It was amazing."

"It was cool, wasn't it? Particularly the landing."

"But I've lost my shoes, or rather his shoes."

"Ah, shoes. I'm afraid they've gone."

"I've got other pairs," Charles said. "I'm glad that you're just safe, and alive."

"Do you have a name?" Joe asked.

"Glin of the Glen."

Both boys laughed.

"Actually, I'm Brack."

"That's a better name." Joe said. "And thank you."

"Thanks?" queried Brack.

"For saving my life."

"You're still an idiot."

"An idiot?"

"For going into the bog in the first place."

"Why are you here on your own? Are there any more Goblins here?" Joe asked.

"I was banished, sent here because I did something wrong. I won't tell you the story, but I took the side of a human against a powerful Goblin, which is against Goblin rules."

"But aren't you lonely?"

"I'm not alone, there are fairies and elves, they live in that forest over there."

"You mean the one with the pine trees?" Charles asked.

"No, to the back of it, there is an ancient forest, that is where they live."

"So, we can go and see them", Charles said excitedly.

"Oh no, they are invisible to humans. I mean they don't show themselves."

"But you do".

"Oh, I can make myself disappear, just like this."

"Minx does that." Joe observed.

"Where's he gone?" Charles commented.

"Brack, Brack." Joe called, but there was no answer.

A shoeless Joe (Charles) and Charles returned to the holiday cottage, hoping to sneak into their room without anyone noticing.

"Charles." His mum had spotted him. "Why do you look such a mess? And where are your shoes?"

"Sorry, I fell into a bog, and got all muddy. My shoes disappeared when I got out."

"How can you be so dirty? Go to the washing machine now, leave your clothes there, and go and have a shower, immediately. And Joe?"

"Yes."

"Why are you walking in with dirty shoes? Take them off at once."

"Sorry mum."

"I'm not your mum, what are you thinking?"

"I meant, my mum tells me off for doing the same thing," Joe replied quickly.

When they were changed, showered and safe, within the four walls of the cottage, both boys decided they were not going to go back to the bog. They had been terrified by the Boggart. If anyone had told them two months ago that Goblins, Fairies, Elves and terrifying Boggarts existed, they would have just laughed.

Over the two weeks, they scrambled up hills, visited castles, swam in a Loch, played cards and lots of other games. Joe chose some gifts for Maggie and his mum, with some money from Charles' pocket money, ate too much fudge and Edinburgh rock, which he actually found too sickly.

The 26th of August seemed a long way away, but each boy was counting down the days in their mind. Joe, also on a piece of paper.

Sometimes, as they ran, played, climbed, they almost forgot who they really were, and how short a time it was.

Charles' parents didn't really notice, except they sensed the change, but put it down to the influence Joe, the other boy. Lucy, preferred her brother like this, as he was much nicer to her. They thought that Charles had become more observant than he had been and much politer. Joe impressed them by how easily he fitted in. If they had known the truth and believed it, they would have been very surprised.

Joe was enjoying himself, the freedom, the wild places. He knew this experience might never happen again, unless Charles remained a friend, perhaps.

They travelled back on the 24th of August, both boys anxious about the next two days.

Chapter 9 - I'M HOME

The morning of the 26th arrived.

The two boys met up at the park. They wanted to see Minx. It was pouring with rain. Both boys had put on black trousers and black raincoats, hoods up.

When Minx appeared, she couldn't tell them apart.

"Can't you make the rain stop?" Joe asked.

"No, that isn't in my gift. Why did you call?"

"Today's the day we switch back."

"Oh yes, so it is."

"When?" Charles asked.

"Sometime." Minx answered. She pointed up the hill. "I've got to go; as there's some pompous guy who lives up there. He's so annoying. I don't know how his wife puts up with him, or anyone else. I play tricks on him, the funniest one is when he listens to Radio 4, and it suddenly changes to Radio 1. It annoys him so much. Then I changed the colour of his underpants from black to red. It's fun to play tricks on him. He's some sort of government man."

"But will it happen soon?" Joe asked.

"I may be a trickster, a Goblin. But if I say it's going to happen, it will." With that, Minx disappeared.

"What shall we do?" Charles moaned.

"Get a burger and chips. I'm hungry."

"Have you got any money?"

"From your allowance. Oh, by the way I didn't take it all. You'll find an envelope in your drawer with quite a bit left of your allowance."

"Thanks."

They went out for burger and chips. Time seeming to pass slowly, as it does when you want time to pass quickly. Then they watched out of the window of the café as the rain cloud passed. Gradually the umbrellas were put away and although the sun didn't shine it stayed drier.

They found a bench, overlooking the town, from the top of a hill, and waited.

Then something shifted, inside of them.

"It's happened. I'm back. We're back." Joe shouted excitedly. "I'm me, and it just happened. I didn't even feel dizzy or anything."

Charles pinched himself. "Yes, I'm me."

"How was it, being me?" he asked.

"Well, a Summer in your shoes was certainly an experience….that…I don't want to do again."

"But we can still be friends."

"Yes, friends."

"What are you going to do now?"

"Go home, back to the life I know."

"But it won't ever be the same again."

"No."

"Call me, you've got my number."

"Yes."

They still sat on the bench.

"We've been close, haven't we?" Joe observed.

"Yes."

"Closer than brothers?"

"Yes."

"Well, bye."

Charles got up and went down the hill to his home. A big black car passed him, driving through a large puddle, next to where Charles was walking on the pavement. Charles was already wet from the rain. The extra soaking from the speeding car almost went almost unnoticed. He didn't feel the same person as he was before. He wanted to be able to sit with his parents and watch TV, play with Lucy. Study better at school, to eat more burgers and chips, and spend less time in his room, on his own. The cascade of water from the bow wave, caused by the wheels, didn't annoy him as it might have done.

Joe stayed a few moments as he watched Charles disappear round a corner, then got up and left himself.

"Mum, I'm home." Both boys called out as they came through their front door.

Minx smiled, as she watched them in the magic bubble she created. Humans, she thought, some aren't so bad. She then thought of Sneaky. Would he really report her to the Goblin Lords. What they didn't need was some official Goblin coming to their town, and interfering.

She then went to the annoying government guy's house, as a big black, important car came and drove him away. Someone needs to teach you a lesson, she thought. I wonder how? What mischief can I do, that's more trouble than I have done so far? With that she flitted away.

www.ingramcontent.com/pod-product-compliance
Lightning Source LLC
Chambersburg PA
CBHW061224070526
44584CB00029B/3969